Lil' Pinoy Explorers'

BISAYA

Written and Illustrated by

Mary Repollo

Copyright © 2024 by Mary Repollo.

All rights reserved.

No part of this publication may be reproduced, distributed, or transmitted in any form or by any means, including photocopying, recording, or other electronic or mechanical methods, without the prior written permission of the publisher, except in the case of brief quotations embodied in critical reviews and certain other noncommercial uses permitted by copyright law. For permission requests, write to the publisher, addressed "Attention: Permissions Coordinator," at repollomary17@gmail.com.

Any facts provided in this book has been checked for accuracy from the time of publication.

Written and Illustrated by Mary Repollo

First printing edition 2024.

ISBN: 978-0-6458805-0-2

Acknowledgement

To everyone who bought the book, thank you so much for your support. It means so much to me that you enjoy and use this book for your little ones to learn more about being Bisaya and Filipino.

Dedication

I want to dedicate this book to my daughter, Valia. She never fails to remind me that I need to keep doing this so she can learn her roots.

I also want to thank my husband, Vincent, who has been patient with me throughout this process. Your support is why I've managed to achieve so much.

To my son, I'm hoping that one day you would be interested enough to learn more about your cultural heritage.

Quick Message

Studies have shown that children who are aware of their cultural identity thrive better.

I have been faced with questions regarding being Filipino and the Philippines in general from two very curious kids. After failing to find books for my kids online, I decided to embark on a journey of rediscovering the Filipino culture and sharing it with other parents who have curious little explorers.

This book is part of a series that I'm working on to help our migrant children learn about being a Filipino and being Bisaya. Read together with your kids and bond with them as you introduce the Bisaya language and open up a whole new world for them to explore!

Mary Repollo

English

Soursop

Bisaya

Guyabano
gu-yah-bah-noh

In some cultures, different parts of the soursop tree, such as the seeds, leaves, and bark, were used in herbal remedies. People believed that it helped with various ailments like headaches, cancer and high blood pressure. So, soursop is not just a tasty fruit, but it is also valued for its potential health benefits throughout history.

English

Bisaya

Avocado

Abokado

ah-bu-kah-doh

Another name for avocados are "alligator pears". This is due to their tough, bumpy skin that looks very similar to an alligator's scales. So, the next time you see an avocado, you can imagine that you're holding a little alligator pear in your hands!

English
Custard Apple

Bisaya
Atis
ah-tis

Custard apple is often referred to as the "Buddha's head fruit" due to its unique appearance. It has a bumpy and irregular shape, resembling the texture of a brain or the head of a statue. Beyond its peculiar appearance, custard apples are known for their creamy, custard-like texture and sweet flavor. Let's try some together!

Did you know that guavas are called "super fruits"? They earned this nickname because they are packed with lots of vitamins and nutrients that are super good for our bodies! Guavas are especially rich in vitamin C, which helps keep our immune system strong and helps us fight off germs and stay healthy.

English
Guava

Bisaya
Bayabas
bah-yah-bas

Did you know that pomelos are the giants of the citrus fruit family? They are the largest citrus fruits in the world. Some pomelos can grow to be as big as a small bowling bowl. Just imagine holding and eating a fruit that's that big!

English
Pomelo

Bisaya
Boongon
bu-u-ngun

English
Calamondin

Bisaya
Limonsito
li-mun-si-to

Did you know that *lemonsito* is a magical fruit that can make your hair shine and clean your scalp? Some people use calamondin juice as a natural hair rinse to make their hair look extra shiny and healthy. It's like a secret beauty trick hidden in a tiny fruit!

English
Starfruit

Bisaya
Carambola
kah-rahm-bu-lah

The starfruit was named for the star-shaped pattern found in its center, which is unlike any other fruit. They are not only fun to look at, but they are also tasty to eat. They have a sweet and tangy flavor. Some people even describe them as tasting like a combination of apples, grapes, and citrus fruits.

English
Bisaya

Durian
Duryan
dur-yan

Did you know that durian is the "king of fruits"? It's known for its spiky exterior and powerful aroma that some people say smells like a mix of sweet, custardy goodness and a little bit of stink! While the smell might be strong, many people actually love the taste of durian and consider durian *pastillas* as a special treat.

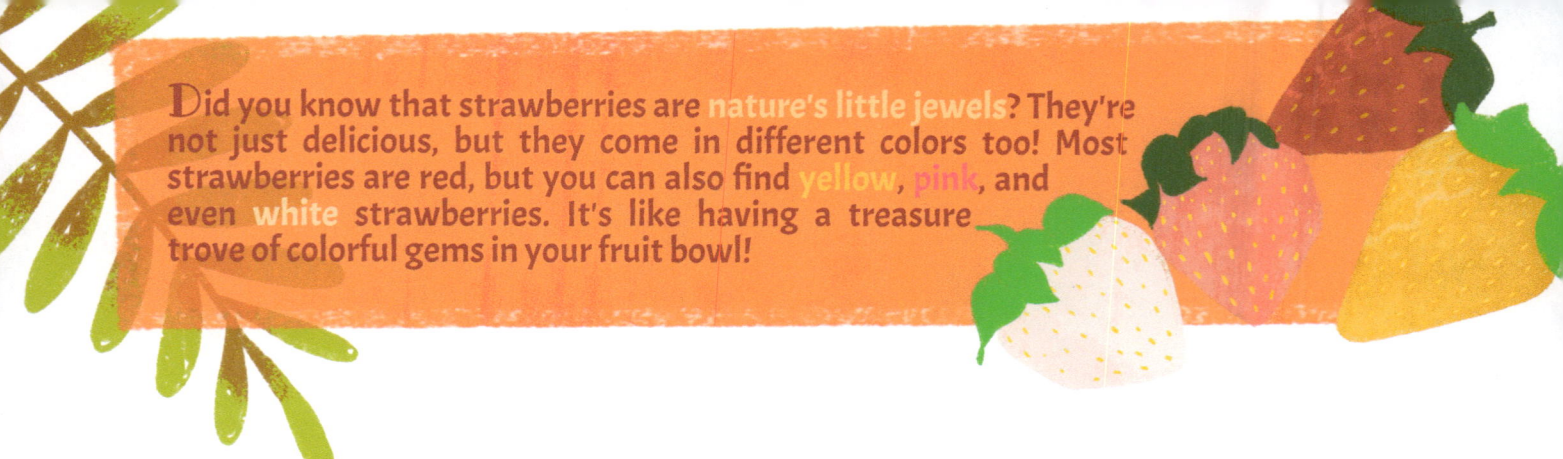

Did you know that strawberries are nature's little jewels? They're not just delicious, but they come in different colors too! Most strawberries are red, but you can also find yellow, pink, and even white strawberries. It's like having a treasure trove of colorful gems in your fruit bowl!

English
Strawberry

Bisaya
Istroberi
ees-troh-beh-ri

English	Bisaya
Orange	**Kahel**
	kah-hel

Did you know that oranges were once considered luxury items? Back in ancient times, oranges were rare and precious fruits. They were so special that they were given as gifts to kings and queens! It wasn't until later that oranges became widely available and enjoyed by people around the world. When you bite into a juicy orange, remember its royal history and savor the taste of this once highly-prized fruit!

English

Bisaya

Tomatoes

Kamatis
kah-mah-tis

Did you know that tomatoes are little red powerhouses of goodness? They are packed with a special nutrient called lycopene, which gives them their bright red color. Lycopene is like a secret weapon for your body — it helps keep your heart strong and healthy!

Did you know that chestnuts are called the "bread of the poor"? Before modern farming techniques and widespread access to food, chestnuts were a staple food for many people, especially in Europe. They were abundant and could be harvested in large quantities, making them an affordable and nutritious option. They were ground into flour and used to make bread, porridge, and other dishes.

English
Chestnuts

Bisaya
Kastanyas
kah-stah-nyas

English

Lychee

Bisaya

Letsiyas
let-see-yas

Lychee seeds have been found preserved in **ancient Chinese tombs** dating back thousands of years. But here's the intriguing part – some people believe that these seeds have the power to bring good luck and ward off evil spirits! So, the next time you enjoy a lychee, remember that you're not just savoring its deliciousness, but also carrying a piece of ancient folklore and fortune!

Did you know that coconuts have three cool parts? First, there's the refreshing coconut water, like a natural drink straight from paradise. Then, there's the creamy white flesh, perfect for yummy recipes. And to top it off, the hard shell makes a great percussion instrument for a tropical band! Coconuts are full of surprises, taste delicious, and even provide a beat. So grab a coconut, have a sip, a bite, and create some musical island vibes!

English
Coconut

Bisaya
Lubi
lu-bi

Jambolan plums have been used in traditional medicine to help *regulate blood sugar levels*. The seeds of the jambolan plum contain compounds that may have a beneficial impact on blood sugar control. Isn't that amazing? So, the next time you enjoy a jambolan plum, remember its hidden powers and the ancient wisdom it holds!

English
Jambolan Plums

Bisaya
Lumboy
lum-boy

English

Java Apple

Bisaya

Makopa
mah-koh-pah

Java apple grows best in lower altitudes with a more dry tropical climate. It is often confused with another similar fruit — tambis. When you take a bite, you'll discover a crisp and refreshing taste that's like a fruity adventure for your taste buds. Grab a Java apple and let your imagination go wild in the warm tropical jungles!

English

Mango

Bisaya

Mangga

mahng-gah

Mangoes are fruits with a fascinating travel history! They were introduced to the Americas by Portuguese explorers in the 16th century. From there, they spread to the Caribbean and reached Florida in the United States. Today, mangoes are not only loved in their native regions but also enjoyed by people in far-flung places. Delicious!

During the 19th century, Queen Victoria of England developed a fascination for mangosteen after hearing about its **unique flavor and medicinal properties**. The story goes that Queen Victoria offered a reward to anyone who could successfully deliver her a fresh mangosteen fruit. However, due to the long journey and perishable nature of the fruit, no one succeeded. This incident made it more popular, cementing its status as a fruit fit for a queen!

English
Mangosteen

Bisaya
Mangostan
mang-gus-stahn

English

Apple

Bisaya

Mansanas
man-sah-nas

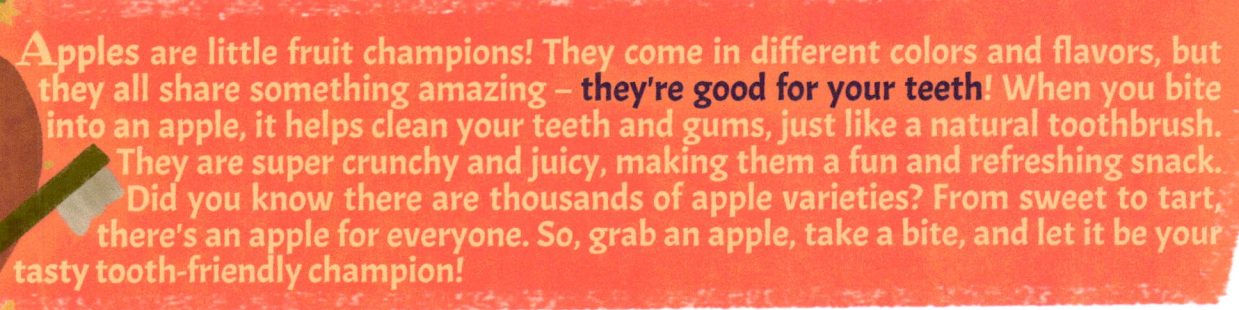

Apples are little fruit champions! They come in different colors and flavors, but they all share something amazing – **they're good for your teeth**! When you bite into an apple, it helps clean your teeth and gums, just like a natural toothbrush. They are super crunchy and juicy, making them a fun and refreshing snack. Did you know there are thousands of apple varieties? From sweet to tart, there's an apple for everyone. So, grab an apple, take a bite, and let it be your tasty tooth-friendly champion!

English
Rockmelon

Bisaya
Melon
meh-lon

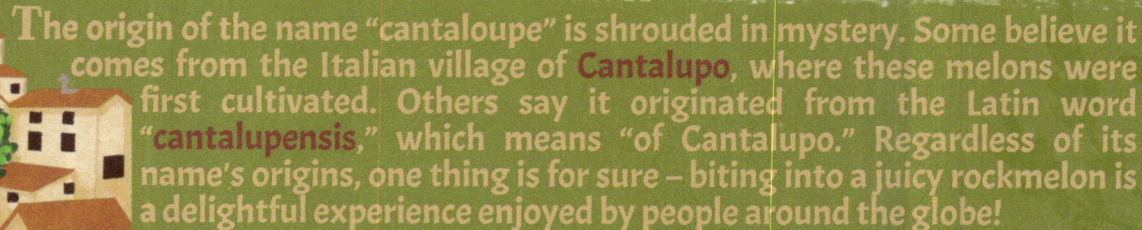

The origin of the name "cantaloupe" is shrouded in mystery. Some believe it comes from the Italian village of **Cantalupo**, where these melons were first cultivated. Others say it originated from the Latin word "**cantalupensis**," which means "of Cantalupo." Regardless of its name's origins, one thing is for sure – biting into a juicy rockmelon is a delightful experience enjoyed by people around the globe!

Did you know that jackfruit seeds are **edible**? In some cultures, they are boiled or roasted and enjoyed as a nutritious snack or used as an ingredient in various recipes. They have a nutty flavor and can be used in both savory and sweet dishes. So, the next time you enjoy a delicious serving of jackfruit, remember that there's more to this fruit than meets the eye – its seeds hold a tasty surprise!

English

Jackfruit

Bisaya

Nangka
nang-kah

Did you know that watermelons have been cultivated for thousands of years? Archaeologists have discovered evidence of watermelon in ancient Egyptian tombs, suggesting that this refreshing fruit has been enjoyed for millennia. In ancient times, watermelons had a more bitter taste and were primarily used for their hydrating properties. Over centuries of selective breeding, watermelons evolved into the deliciously sweet and refreshing fruit we savor today!

English

Bisaya

Watermelon

Pakwan

pah-kwan

English

Papaya

Bisaya

Kapayas
kah-pah-yas

Papaya is a tropical wonder fruit! It has a special enzyme called papain that helps break down food in your tummy. It's a little helper for your digestion! Papaya is also packed with vitamins and antioxidants that are great for your body. So, the next time you enjoy a slice of papaya, imagine you're savoring a tropical treasure that keeps your tummy happy and your body healthy!

Pears are the superheroes of the fruit world! They may not wear capes, but they're packed with fiber and nutrients that help keep your body strong and healthy. Did you know that pears are also great for your tummy? They have a special kind of fiber called **pectin** that helps with digestion and keeps things moving smoothly. So, the next time you bite into a juicy pear, imagine yourself becoming a superhero with a mighty and happy tummy, ready to take on any adventure.

English

Pears

Bisaya

Peras
peh-ras

The pineapple is a tropical crowned jewel with its spiky exterior and vibrant yellow flesh. But here's the surprising part – pineapple is the only fruit that contains an enzyme called **bromelain**. It helps break down food and makes it easier for your body to digest. Pineapple is also packed with vitamins and antioxidants that are great for your body. So, the next time you enjoy a slice of pineapple, imagine yourself wearing a fruity crown and feeling like a tropical king or queen!

English
Pineapple

Bisaya
Pinya
pin-yah

English

Rambutan

Bisaya

Rambutan
rahm-boo-tahn

Rambutan is a fruit that wears a spiky hairstyle. The name "rambutan" actually comes from the Malay-Indonesian word "rambut," which means "hair." When you look at a rambutan fruit, you'll notice its vibrant, hairy outer covering, resembling a burst of colorful hair. But here's the interesting part – those spiky hairs are not just for show! They serve a purpose of protecting the fruit inside. Once you peel away the hairy exterior, you'll find a juicy, sweet, and translucent flesh that sweet and tasty!

English

Banana

Bisaya

Saging
sah-ging

Bananas have an interesting relationship with gravity. When bananas grow, they exhibit a unique behavior known as "negative geotropism." Unlike most fruits that hang downwards, bananas grow towards the sun, defying gravity and curving upwards. This gives bananas their distinct curvature. So when you hold a banana, marvel at its graceful curve and remember its fascinating response to the pull of the Earth's gravitational force!

English
Bisaya

Tamarind
Sambag
sahm-bahg

Tamarind is like a zesty time traveler! It has been enjoyed for thousands of years in different parts of the world. People love its unique flavor that's both tangy and sweet. But here's the fascinating part – tamarind has a special place in history too! It was often used in traditional medicines and even as a natural dye for coloring clothes. It is like a magical fruit that brings flavor and color to the world!

Water apple, also known as **rose apple**, is a fruit that contains various vitamins and minerals. While the exact vitamin content may vary slightly, water apple is particularly rich in **vitamin C**. It is an essential nutrient that plays a vital role in supporting the immune system, promoting healthy skin, and aiding in the absorption of iron.

English

Water Apple

Bisaya

Tambis
tahm-bis

English
Grapes

Bisaya
Ubas
oo-bahs

In Greek mythology, grapes were associated with Dionysus, the god of wine and celebration. According to legend, Dionysus created grapes and taught mortals the art of winemaking. They were considered a sacred fruit associated with festivities, joy, and the pleasures of life. Today, grapes are enjoyed fresh, dried as raisins, and transformed into delightful wines. Cheers!

Humana!
hoo-mah-nah

The End!

www.ingramcontent.com/pod-product-compliance
Lightning Source LLC
Chambersburg PA
CBHW041200290426
44109CB00002B/76